Seeds

By
Gemma McMullen

Contents

Page 4   What is a Plant?
Page 6   What are Seeds?
Page 8   What do Seeds Do?
Page 10   What do Seeds look Like?
Page 12   Fruity Seeds?
Page 14   How do People use Seeds?
Page 16   Other uses for Seeds
Page 18   Clever Plants
Page 20   Seeds on the Move
Page 22   Seed Secrets
Page 24   Glossary and Index

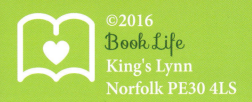

©2016
Book Life
King's Lynn
Norfolk PE30 4LS

ISBN: 978-1-910512-50-0

Written by
Gemma McMullen

Edited by
Amy Allatson

Designed by
Ian McMullen

Words that appear like *this* can be found in the glossary on page 24.

What is a Plant?

A plant is a living thing. Trees, shrubs, flowers and weeds are all plants. People and animals need plants to live.

A Plant

Sunlight

Plants need water, sunlight and heat to live. They make their own food using energy from the Sun.

What are Seeds?

Seed

All plants have different parts. Seeds are parts of the plant. Not all plants make seeds.

Some seeds are large and easy to see, some seeds are very small. Different plants make different numbers of seeds.

Mustard Seed

Coconut Seed

7

What do Seeds Do?

Plants make seeds so that more plants can grow. Inside each seed is a new plant.

Dandelion Seed

The hard shell of a seed *protects* it until the seed has all of the things that it needs to grow.

Conker Seed

9

What do Seeds look Like?

There are lots of types of seeds and they all look different. They can be lots of shapes and sizes.

Poppy seeds are small seeds that are black in colour.

Poppy Seeds

Avocado seeds are much larger. They are inside the fruit.

Avocado Seed

Fruity Seeds

Strawberry seeds are small and yellow. They are found on the outside of the fruit.

Strawberry Seeds

Apple Seeds

Apple seeds are found on the inside of the fruit. Apple seeds are brown.

How many fruits can you think of that have seeds inside them?

How do People use Seeds?

Some seeds are *edible* for humans, which means that they can be eaten. Beans are seeds which are popular foods.

Baked Beans

Broad Beans

Sunflower seeds have oil inside them which can be used for cooking.

Sunflower Seeds

Sesame Seeds

Sesame seeds are often sprinkled on top of bread rolls.

Other uses for Seeds

Gardeners use seeds to grow new plants.
They can choose which plants they have in their gardens.

Planting
Seeds

Many people choose to grow vegetables. They plant seeds which grow into plants that they can eat.

Clever Plants

Plants make lots of seeds so that there is a good chance that some will grow into new plants.

The sunflower is made up of lots of tiny flowers which all turn into seeds

The seeds move away from the *parent plant* in different ways. This is to give them the best chance of *survival*.

A dandelion flower uses wind to move its seeds.

A sycamore seed spins away like a helicopter from the parent plant.

19

Seeds on the Move

Some fruits with seeds inside drop off the tree. They are often round in shape so that they can roll away from the parent plant.

Apples roll away.

Some seeds stick to passing animals, sooner or later dropping off in a new place.

A Spiky
Burdock Seed

Seed Secrets

Coco-not!
Did you know that a coconut is actually a seed, not a nut?

Pea Shooter
Pea pods split and fire their seeds out!

Poo Planting!

Some seeds are kept inside fruits and berries. Birds eat the fruit then pass out the seeds, which can still grow.

Glossary

edible can be eaten safely

parent plant the plant from where they came

protects keeps safe from harm

survival to carry on living

Index

apple 12, 20

avocado seeds 11

beans 14

plant 4, 5, 6, 7, 8, 16, 17, 18, 19, 20

poppy seeds 11

sesame seeds 15

strawberry seeds 12

sunflower seeds 15, 18

Photo Credits

Photocredits: Abbreviations: l-left, r-right, b-bottom, t-top, c-centre, m-middle. All images are courtesy of Shutterstock.com.

Front Cover – Singkham. Front Cover inset – racorn. 2-3 – Singkham. 4 – Kevin Shine. 5 – Tom Wang. 6 – Richard Griffin. 7 – Africa Studio. 7inset – ptnphoto. 8 – sss615. 9 – Kostiantyn Fastov. 9inset – Andris Tkacenko. 10 – Monika Gniot. 10inset, 24 – Valentina Razumova. 11 – leonori. 12 – Tomsickova Tatyana. 13 – Whiteaster. 14 – Robert Anthony. 14inset – eZeePics. 15 – In Green. 15inset – SMarina. 16 – Brian Goodman. 17 – michaeljung. 18 – valeriiaarnaud. 18inset – In Green. 19 – Brian A Jackson. 19linset – Sue Robinson. 19minset – joannawnuk. 20 – Vasily Mulyukin. 20inset – Foxxy63. 21 – Vitaly Ilyasov. 22 – S_Photo. 22inset – Dionisvera. 23bl – Tim UR. 23 – Maksimilian. 23trinset – Kant Komalasnangkoon.